CU00867347

BRAIN LIKE TWAIN

TWAIN

**Improve Your Writing Skills in 30 Days
Using Mark Twain's Secret Methods**

DAVID ANDREW LLOYD
With Mark Twain*

HOW TO USE THIS BOOK

Success in 30 Days

By reading a Tip-A-Day (and doing the *Brain Like Twain* assignments at the end of each chapter), you will master some of the tricks Mark Twain used to become one of America's most popular and prolific authors.

The book is divided into three main parts with 10 tips per part. First, as Huck Finn might say, you'll find *Basic Ritin' Lessons*, then *Advanced Ritin' Tricks*, and finally *Sum Serius Literacy Technik* to polish your pen.

At the end, you will find *Ten Bonus Tips* for you overachievers (and you know who you are).

Or Genius in a Week

Short on time? Try our "Turbo Process." Read five short chapters a day and select one of the assignments to develop your *Brain Like Twain* in only one week – but we suggest you recharge your mind periodically (see below).

Reset, Recharge & Repeat

As a refresher, perform the "Turbo Process" above six months after your initial reading. Then you can reset your brain every year or two, or whenever Halley's Comet returns, whichever comes sooner.

Oh, one more thing… for anyone expecting one of those long-winded, tedious prefaces, introductions or acknowledgements, this was it.

INTRODUCTION

Mark Twain was born Samuel Clemens, but shall be referred to as Twain throughout this book to reduce any confusion.

From Pauper to Literary Prince

Although *The Celebrated Jumping Frog of Calaveras County* gained Twain national recognition, his humorous stories had already been entertaining readers in Nevada and San Francisco, where he was a newspaper reporter.

In 1866, the *Sacramento Daily Union* hired him to write a series of articles on Hawaii (known as the Sandwich Islands at that time). Since his comic style became instantly popular, a friend convinced him to begin a lecture tour, and people packed theaters to hear his humorous travel stories.

The following year, Twain convinced the *Daily Alta California* to pay for his passage on the *Quaker City,* a steamship tour to Europe and the Holy Land. The paper printed fifty-one of his letters, which became the basis for his first book, *Innocents Abroad.*

In 1876, Twain published *Tom Sawyer,* which became an instant success. Seven years later, he wrote *Adventures of Huckleberry Finn*, which Ernest Hemmingway considered the beginning of all modern American literature.

Twain's insightful humor could rival the biting satire of Voltaire, Swift and other European masters. "I am a great and sublime fool," Twain wrote, "but then I am God's fool, and all His works must be contemplated with respect."

~ Please enjoy Twain's timeline at the end of the book ~

CONTENTS

PART I

Basic Ritin' Lessons
~ Huck Finn

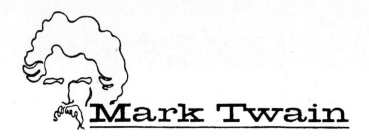

Mark Twain

"Clothes make the man. Naked people have little or no influence on society."

~ *Mark Twain*

Laugh At Yourself
— Before Others Do

To make his characters truly authentic, Mark Twain used a simple, but reliable model: Himself.

He knew he had all the same vices, virtues, imperfections, flaws, and contemptible habits as everyone else.

> I am the whole human race without a detail lacking…
> in myself I find in big or little proportion every quality
> and every defect that is findable in the mass of the race.
> *Mark Twain In Eruption*

Operating on the premise that mankind was a parade of cowards, fools and idiots, Twain believed he was not only marching in the procession, but proudly carrying a banner.

Psychologists might find this inferiority complex debilitating, but, for a writer, it's pure gold. Understanding human nature from this perspective allowed Twain to mine the darkest depths of the human soul without even leaving his own desk – until tea time.

BRAIN LIKE TWAIN

Using the humorous vein of Mark Twain, write a couple paragraphs about yourself, poking fun at your own faults.

[AUTHOR'S NOTE: Then show your work to a few friends and see if they laugh at your skillful eloquence – or your obvious omissions.]

Mark Twain

"The man with a new idea is a
Crank until the idea succeeds."
                        ~ Mark Twain

Take Note

After steamboat pilot Horace Bixby accused a young Twain of not knowing "enough to pilot a cow down a lane," he urged his inexperienced apprentice to jot down every detail about the river in a little notebook.

These notes helped Twain reconstruct his memories for *Life on the Mississippi*, and this practice also helped him develop a habit of writing down his observations.

Twain detested journals, however. He preferred fragments. After hearing an old-timer tell a tall tale at a mining camp, Twain scribbled a few random thoughts that eventually evolved into *The Celebrated Jumping Frog of Calaveras County,* the story that made him famous.

With the invention of computers, some may speculate that Twain would transfer his notes to data files, but he had enough trouble with the typewriter. Besides, he would be over 175 years old and reluctant to change.

BRAIN LIKE TWAIN

Carry a notebook with you today to write down random thoughts. Focus on writing fragments of three or four words. Then review your indiscernible scratches tonight, and see if the words ignite your memory.

[AUTHOR'S NOTE: Keep a notebook by your bed. Ideas have been known to attack writers in their sleep.]

"When in doubt, tell the truth."
~ *Mark Twain*

DAY 3
Be a Know-It-All

Life on the Mississippi remains one of Twain's most enduring works. Rich in detail, full of robust adventure, it was a subject Twain knew extremely well.

> If you attempt to create & build a wholly imaginary incident, adventure or situation, you will go astray, & the artificiality of the thing will be detectable. But if you [focus] on a fact in your personal experience it is an acorn, a root, & every created adornment that grows up out of it & spreads its foliage & blossoms to the sun will seem realities, not inventions. You will not likely to go astray, your compass of fact is there to keep you on the right course."
>
> *Twain's Notebook*

Returning to the river later in life, he was inspired to finish *Huckleberry Finn* with renewed energy and wrote "eight or nine hundred pages in such a brief space of time that I mustn't name the number of days." When Twain tackled a subject he understood clearly, he could get so wrapped up in his writing that he wouldn't even realize he was working.

BRAIN LIKE TWAIN

Focusing on something you know extremely well, write a few paragraphs. Feel the energy as your confidence in the subject propels you forward.

Mark Twain

"Hain't we got all the fools in town on our side? And ain't that a big enough majority in any town?"

~ Mark Twain

DAY 4

Exploit Your Own Childish Behavior

Many of Twain's plots, themes and characters were mined from the rich veins of his own memory.

Some of these recollections were altered, molded and eventually transferred into his work – playful pranks and boyhood adventures; riding the river and exploring caves.

His neighbors, friends and relatives from Hannibal, Missouri became characters in his stories.

In *The Adventures of Tom Sawyer,* fond memories of a childhood sweetheart inspired Becky Thatcher's character.

Aunt Polly was based on Twain's mother, Judge Thatcher was modeled after his father, and Huckleberry Finn personified Tom Blankenship, the kind-hearted son of the town drunk.

BRAIN LIKE TWAIN

Using your friends as characters, write a one-page story about floating down the Mississippi in a raft. What happens to that raft is up to you.

Mark Twain

"Let us be thankful for the fools; but for them the rest of us could not succeed."

~ Mark Twain

Study People

Twain's stories resonate with readers because everyone has encountered similar characters in their own lives.

His secret? Observation.

While working as a steamboat pilot, Twain encountered people from every aspect of life along the banks of the Mississippi.

He had a chance to study the behavior of every scoundrel, drifter, hustler, cheat, dreamer, schemer, swindler, crook, creature, con, coward, drunkard, rascal, hypocrite and, as he liked to say, "quite picturesque liar."

> In that brief, sharp schooling, I got personally and familiarly acquainted with about all the different types of human nature that are to be found in fiction, biography, or history.
>
> *Life on the Mississippi*

So, why are you complaining about your day job? Consider it research. Twain did. Observe the habits of the people you interact with and take mental notes.

BRAIN LIKE TWAIN

Mixing the traits of several people you know, write a short biography for a potential character. Include personal background, ancestry, beliefs, and habits.

"Few things are harder to put up with than the annoyance of a good example."

~ *Mark Twain*

Twain always had a knack for getting into mischief with his writing.

While working as a printer's apprentice, one of Twain's antics almost got him shot. When his brother Orion left town on business, he put young Twain in charge of printing *The Weekly Hannibal Journal.*

Twain decided to write a short article making fun of Higgins, a competing editor. The story was so scathing that Higgins came looking for the young author with a shotgun – until he realized the culprit was a mere boy of thirteen.

Years later, after following his brother Orion to Nevada, Twain periodically wrote humorous letters to the editor of the *Territorial Enterprise* until his persistence earned him a job as a reporter for $5 a day.

Combing the city for news, he found himself writing every day. When he couldn't find anything juicy, he often stretched the truth completely, including the story of a "Petrified Man" who was unearthed in the hills in the "Thinking Man" pose. Most readers caught the clue. Some didn't. Either way, Twain was getting practice.

BRAIN LIKE TWAIN

Choose a subject you're passionate about, and write a letter to the editor on the topic. Try a smaller community paper first because there is less competition.

Mark Twain

"Get your facts first, and then you can distort them as much as you please."

~ Mark Twain

Research Like a Reporter

While working as a reporter in Nevada, Twain was constantly looking for stories to entertain and enlighten his readers.

Sure, he often twisted the truth into unrecognizable distortions, but he started with the facts. Usually.

It's difficult to say what happened to those facts as Twain minced their essence, stewed them in his imagination, and eventually processed them through his warped-but-fertile mind – but the results were often very tasty and readers devoured every morsel with the healthy appetite of hungry cannibals.

As he matured as a writer, Twain later incorporated news articles of the day and references from classic authors (Nietzsche, Darwin, Shakespeare) to build his case and broaden the depth of his stories.

In other words, Twain worked hard to make us laugh.

BRAIN LIKE TWAIN

Read today's paper and pick three to five articles with potential for a short story. Then narrow down your list to write one good story.

[AUTHOR'S NOTE: For example, although we have no evidence, we believe Twain's "Petrified Man" (Day 5) was probably inspired by something actually dug out of the ground near one of the local mining towns.]

Mark Twain

"The time to begin writing an article is when you have finished it to your satisfaction."

~ *Mark Twain*

Finish Your Story
Before You Write It

To create his best work, Twain let his ideas simmer, stew and ferment in his fertile mind until they had enough substance to seep up to the surface on their own.

After a friend lent him a copy of Malory's *Le Morte d'Arthur* in 1884, Twain immediately saw the humor between the restrictions of Medieval conventions and the need for modern conveniences:

> No pockets in the armour. No way to manage certain requirements of nature. Can't scratch. Cold in the head – can't blow – can't get hankerchief, can't use iron sleeve. Iron gets red hot in the sun – leaks in the rain, gets white from frost and freezes me solid in winter. Suffer from lice and fleas. Make disagreeable clatter when I enter church. Can't dress or undress myself. Always getting struck by lighting...
>
> *Twain's Notebook*

Notice how his mind changed direction. After observing that he can't wipe a runny nose with *iron,* he suddenly realizes why modern tailors seldom use metal as a fabric.

BRAIN LIKE TWAIN

Write an outline for a story you've been thinking about. You don't need to be extensive on this assignment, but make sure you have *a beginning, a middle* and *an end.*

Mark Twain

"Nothing so needs reforming as other people's habits."

~ *Mark Twain*

DAY 9
Creating an Awesome Routine

Creative people tend to be the most productive in the early morning or late night hours.

When they wake up, their minds are free from the stress and drama of the day. After dark, the quiet, still surroundings produce a soothing, creative atmosphere.

As an added bonus, sound sleep allows your subconscious to sort through your thoughts like a high-speed computer, solving problems with plot, structure and story logic before you even rise from this tranquil state of mind.

Twain took full advantage of this phenomenon. Spending the summers at their Quarry Farm retreat, Twain would start work at 7:30, skip lunch and write into the early afternoon. These were his most productive years.

When writing *Huckleberry Finn,* he was so engrossed in his work that he would write into the night "six days in the week; & once or twice I smooched a Sunday when the boss [his wife] wasn't looking."

BRAIN LIKE TWAIN

Figure out your most productive time to write. Is it the morning or night? Commit to working at least thirty minutes a day during that time period for one full week.

[AUTHOR'S NOTE: Make writing a habit and it will become as routine as brushing your teeth.]

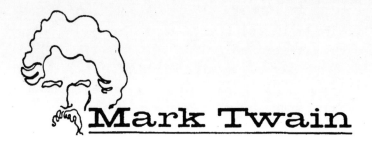

Mark Twain

"The report of my death was an exaggeration."

~ Mark Twain

DAY 10

Solitude: A Lonely But Rewarding Job

Isolation is an essential ingredient for any writing career. It was often solitude and reflection that helped Twain recall the old memories that fueled his imagination.

During the summer, when his family visited their Quarry Farm retreat near Elmira, New York, Twain wrote some of his best work. There were too many distractions in Hartford, with its social scene and visitors interrupting unannounced.

His daughter Clara remembered watching Twain retire to the hilltop pavilion his sister-in-law built for him. Every morning, he would walk out to the octagon-shaped study with "a sheaf of paper under his arm" and "a little caper of delight."

> [The study perched] in complete isolation on top of an elevation that commands leagues of valleys and city and retreating ranges of distant blue hills.
>
> *Letter to a Friend*

The serenity of his hideaway inspired his creative spirit to pen such classics as *Huckleberry Finn*.

BRAIN LIKE TWAIN

Find your happy place. Escape through your bedroom window like Tom Sawyer (or back door if age is creeping up on you). Visit a park, a beach – anywhere nature can nurture you.

PART II

Advanced Ritin' Tricks
- Huck Finn

Mark Twain

"[I] never could make a good impromptu speech without several hours to prepare it."

~ Mark Twain

DAY 11

Ritin' Is Re-Ritin'

During a good summer, Mark Twain could write thousands of words in a single day. However, many of them were never served to the public.

"A successful book," Twain noted, "is not made of what is in it, but what is left out of it."

For Twain, the rewriting process could be a war zone. Papers, pens and notes scattered around like fallen soldiers on a battlefield. Some did not survive, but Twain solemnly honored their sacrifices with stories worthy of their heroic efforts.

> The morning after [the writer] has revised it for the last time & sent it away to the printer…he gets that little shock. All the litter and confusion are gone. The piles of dusty reference-books are gone from the chairs, the maps from the floors; the chaos of letters, manuscripts, note-books…is gone from the writing-table, the furniture is back where it used to be.
>
> *Twain's Memorandum*

BRAIN LIKE TWAIN

Choose one of the previous assignments and rewrite it five times. No, that wasn't a misprint. Print it, mark it up, retype it, repeat. Five times – in succession.

[AUTHOR'S NOTE: Sounds tough, but it's your greatest lesson. You'll be amazed how each draft will differ.]

Mark Twain

"Seventy is old enough. After that there is too much risk."

~ *Mark Twain*

DAY 12

Experience Life

Twain's travel books were one of his most consistent sources of revenue. He simply wrote about his adventures, adding his own humorous twists and observations.

Whenever he was stuck for inspiration, he could also mine material from his early days when he bounced from town to town.

Twain had held a variety of jobs: riverboat pilot, printer, prospector, newspaper reporter, and even a soldier for two weeks during the Civil War, until common sense convinced him to skedaddle and get his hide off the battlefield.

Drawing from this experience, Twain wrote in *The Private History of a Campaign That Failed,* "I knew more about retreating than the man who invented retreating."

> Now then, as the most valuable capital or culture or education usable in the building of novels is personal experience I ought to be well equipped for that trade…and all of it real, none of it artificial…
> *Letter to a Friend, 1891*

BRAIN LIKE TWAIN

Go out and experience something you have never done before – preferably something reasonably sane.

Mark Twain

"Training is everything...the peach was once a bitter almond; cauliflower is nothing but cabbage with a college education."

        ~ Mark Twain

DAY 13

Imitation: Sincerest Form of Flattery

Twain's wildly popular style was little more than the tall tales he learned from the people he meet along the Mississippi.

Applying the same enthralling tone and mesmerizing pace, Twain's stories came alive on the page, making his novels so novel.

When he told stories on stage as a speaker, he added dramatic pauses, as he had learned from the people telling their stories along the Mississippi.

His favorite tale was *The Golden Arm.* As he learned from watching others tell the tale, the pause had to be "timed just right." Never rushed, nor lingering too long.

If· he held the beat "the right length precisely," he could "make some impressible girl deliver a startled little yelp and jump out of her seat" – and that was exactly the response he was after.

BRAIN LIKE TWAIN

Choose one of your favorite Mark Twain stories and type out an entire page on your computer. Feel his style. Notice the rhythm of his words. Appreciate his tone and tempo.

Mark Twain

"Thunder is good, thunder is impressive; but it is lightning that does the work."

~ *Mark Twain*

DAY 14

Turning Your Spark into an Inferno

Anything can provide the inspiration to write, but it's your darned persistence that turns these ideas into gold.

Professional writers wake up every day and work.

In Twain's era, periodicals often paid writers by the word, which explains why some of his stories seem long-winded at times. He was simply paying himself a little overtime.

After writing a series of travel articles for the *Daily Alta California,* he turned the overseas assignment into his first book, *Innocents Abroad.*

Since he had already completed his writing chores, Twain figured he'd sit back, smoke a few cigars, and wait for the cash to roll in on the afternoon stagecoach.

Unfortunately, the publisher wanted several thousand more words. Undaunted, Twain nailed his posterior to his chair until hand cramps took his mind off any potential hemorrhoids – and finished the task in less than two months.

BRAIN LIKE TWAIN

Take the story you outlined in Day 8 and write a few pages in one sitting. Don't look back. Don't worry about grammar, logic or spelling. Just do it. You can edit later.

[AUTHOR'S NOTE: As you learned in Day 11, you can (and should) rewrite everything. So just start writing. You can worry about changes another day.]

Mark Twain

"All you need in life is ignorance and confidence, and then success is sure."

~ Mark Twain

Love Your Work

If you became a writer to make money, you entered the wrong profession.

You must have passion or you'll never be rewarded.

When you write, your words will become diluted twice. First, they will lose some power when you transfer them from your mind to the paper, because the perfect word is an elusive beast.

Then the reader will interpret your work with their own feelings and experiences, weakening your story even further.

Therefore, you need intense passion to make your readers feel a mere tinge of your emotion. To make them shed a single tear, your words must cry uncontrollably. To make them smile, your words must laugh hysterically.

Twain woke up every morning anxious to write. Even when he was not putting his pen to paper, his ideas were marinating in his head.

"The writing of books," Twain wrote, "was always play, not work. I enjoyed it; it was merely billiards to me."

BRAIN LIKE TWAIN

Today you can write a couple pages about anything you want, except a research paper. Nobody likes those darn research papers.

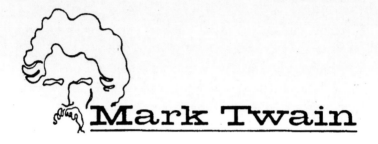

Mark Twain

"Classic. A book which people praise and don't read."

~ Mark Twain

Readin'& Ritin'

Twain supplemented his personal experiences by reading and then reprocessing that material until it seeped out of his head in the form of genius.

When a friend gave him a book about King Arthur, it inspired *A Connecticut Yankee in King Arthur's Court.* In later years, *The Prince and the Pauper, Joan of Arc* and other tales were laced with European references.

Even current events of the time influenced Twain. Before writing *Pudd'nhead Wilson,* Twain fueled his anger by reading reports about the many racially charged trials. News about the U.S. action in the Philippines ignited his anti-imperialistic rage.

During our nation's centennial of 1876, Twain observed people celebrating a century of freedom, but read articles about blacks being denied basic civil liberties. This helped focus his story for *Huckleberry Finn.*

Dickens and other authors may have been more dramatic, but the results were the same. Classic authors decode the news of their era and write social commentary that lasts for eternity.

BRAIN LIKE TWAIN

Recall some books or news reports you have read. Could any inspire a story or supplement something you are presently writing?

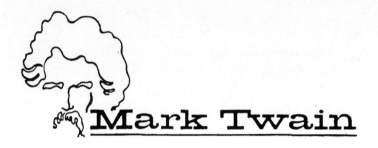

Mark Twain

"[This critic] has pulled out his carving-knife and his tomahawk and is starting after a book which he is going to have for breakfast."
~ Mark Twain

Taking Sides

Have you ever noticed when you have a lover's quarrel or an argument about your favorite sports team, the other person is *always* wrong?

Writers must acknowledge their own prejudices and overcome this tendency to remain objective. For most of the 19th century, slavery was a polarizing subject and Twain artfully showed both sides in *Huck Finn*.

> It most froze me to hear such talk…coming right out flat-footed and saying he would steal his children – children that belonged to a man I didn't even know; a man that hadn't ever done me no harm.
>
> *Adventures of Huckleberry Finn*

Missouri was a slave state when Twain grew up, so he accepted slavery as a normal part of life. However, when he observed the atrocities and injustices, he had his own conflict of conscience.

This explains why it took a Southerner with firsthand knowledge to write one of the greatest arguments against racial injustice.

BRAIN LIKE TWAIN

Take a hot topic (politics, environment, universal health care), and write a paragraph supporting the side you are *least likely* to agree with.

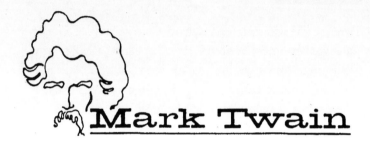

"The difference between the right word and the almost right word is... the difference between lightning and the lightning bug."

~ Mark Twain

K.I.S.S. – Keep It Simple, Sam

Twain's style was simple, direct and unpretentious.

Although he could decorate a story with adjectives and incite fury with his verbs, the words usually went through an extensive screening process before they were offered the job.

In fact, the innocent adjectives were often the first words to get shuffled to the unemployment line. "As to the Adjective," he wrote, "When in doubt, strike it out."

> God only exhibits his thunder and lightning at intervals, and so they always command attention. These are God's adjectives. You thunder and lightning too much; the reader ceases to get under the bed, by and by.
>
> *Letter to his brother Orion*

Always resist the urge of being too formal. "There are no people who are quite so vulgar," Twain observed, "as the over-refined ones."

Be yourself and avoid those fancy words. It worked for Twain.

BRAIN LIKE TWAIN

Taking one of the assignments you've completed (assuming you've been doing your homework), replace all the verbs and adjectives with stronger words. See if you can make it more powerful.

Mark Twain

"Every one is a moon, and has a dark side which he never shows to anybody."

~ *Mark Twain*

DAY 19

A Prescription for Description

Whenever you read anything by Mark Twain, he makes you feel like you're in the story, the water gently splashing against your raft, the smell of farms, animals, and even ham sizzling in a skillet.

People come alive with their features, mannerisms and distinctive speech. His descriptions are as vivid as photographs.

Life on the Mississippi may be one of his richest works to study. As a former steamboat pilot, he knew the great river as a mother would know her own child.

> …great volumes of the blackest smoke are rolling and tumbling out of the chimneys…the pent steam is screaming through the gauge-cocks, the captain lifts his hand, a bell rings, the wheels stop; then they turn back, churning the water to foam…
>
> *Life On The Mississippi*

Calling up memories like a high-speed Internet connection, Twain could spit out details faster than Google, and then paint a dazzling picture, agonizing over every color, shade and tint until the reader could visualize his world in its full glory.

BRAIN LIKE TWAIN

At lunch, observe someone eating their meal and describe their features and mannerisms in detail.

[AUTHOR'S NOTE: If it's good enough, you might get their phone number. If not, they might call the police. Either way, you'll get some action.]

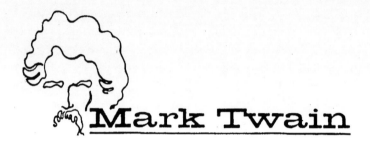

Mark Twain

"It were not best that we should all think alike; it is difference of opinion that makes horse-races."

~ Mark Twain

DAY 20
Getting a Second Opinion

When Twain was a newspaper reporter in the Old West, he had plenty of editors to bully and threaten the emerging talent.

However, when he lived in Hartford, scholars believe he produced his finest work because he was at the mercy of his most brutally honest editor: his wife.

Livy, with her Victorian upbringing, made it her duty to rough out the edges of her "Youth," as she called her husband.

She would sit down on the porch and read Twain's early drafts to their young daughters, and, when she came across a particularly fine passage, as Twain noted, "she would strike it out."

Whenever that happened, though, Twain was often playing a prank on his sweetheart. He knew his daughters would love anything he wrote, so he intentionally inserted a weak line here and there to get a rise out of Livy.

Writers are like masochists. They must seek out their most ruthless friends to review their work. In the long run, brutal honesty from an acquaintance hurts less than a vicious rejection slip from a publisher.

BRAIN LIKE TWAIN

Ask six friends to review your latest project, and tell them to offer you "honest feedback." It might hurt, but it will make you a better writer.

PART III

Serius Stuff
~ Huck Finn

Mark Twain

"Ignorant people think it's the noise which fighting cats make that is so aggravating, but it ain't so; it's the sickening grammar they use."

~ Mark Twain

Specific Words for Specific Reasons

Clarity is essential to help people understand your message.

Resist the urge to use vague words such as "it" or "thing," or even "they" to describe specific items. Replace these empty words with descriptive phrases and memorable details.

Instead of simply writing, "The steamboat arrived at the dock, and the townspeople ran to it," Twain wrote:

> The town drunk stirs…every store and house pours out a human contribution, and all in a twinkling the dead town is alive and moving. Drays, carts, men, boys, all go hurrying from the many quarters to a common center; the wharf.
>
> *Life on the Mississippi*

When effectively used, written words create a movie in the reader's mind. Your audience can practically see the imagery, and feel the people's emotions and thoughts.

BRAIN LIKE TWAIN

Using one of your earlier assignments, replace vague passages with descriptive words, and watch your story evolve.

Mark Twain

*"Everything human is pathetic.
The secret source of Humor is
not joy but sorrow. There is no
humor in heaven."*

~ Mark Twain

Taking Humor Seriously

Although some people condemn humor as an infantile form of literature, Twain elevated it to high art and he remains America's most quoted authority on – everything!

Propelled by his anger, and tempered by his sardonic wit, Twain's scathing observations on society opened our eyes to injustice, corruption, racism and the inadequacy of our own human frailties.

Like the bubbling lava from an active volcano, his satirical words could explode with brutal force, often saying more in one line ("I believe our Heavenly Father invented man because he was disappointed in the monkey") than most authors could say in an entire book (Darwin's *Origin of Species*).

He did not write for the sake of humor. He wrote to make a point. If humor came forth on its own, he would "allow it a place in my sermons."

BRAIN LIKE TWAIN

Take something serious (lost love, physical pain). Focusing only on the humorous side, write down a few observations.

[AUTHOR'S NOTE: Your personal point of view often dictates the humor. If a doctor left a surgical sponge in your body, that would not be funny; but, if they left it inside a fictional patient, it would be hysterical – especially if the hospital charged them extra for the additional procedure.]

Mark Twain

"[Foreign tour] guides can not master the subtleties of the American joke."

~ *Mark Twain*

Adding Punch to Your Punch Lines

Mark Twain used several methods to make his readers smile. One was the *twist* or *zinger*.

Lead your audience in one direction, and then pull the rug out from under them with a surprise at the end. Here are a few of Twain's classics:

1. "Always do right. This will gratify some people, and astonish the rest."
2. "It could probably be shown by facts and figures that there is no distinctly native American criminal class except Congress."
3. "Man is the only animal that blushes. Or needs to."

The twist is always the last part of the sentence, and the final word usually packs the most powerful punch.

One of the easiest ways to learn this trick is by twisting a common cliché such as Twain's, "Familiarity breeds contempt – and children."

Or the opening quote (Day 1) of this book: "Clothes make the man. Naked people have little or no influence on society."

BRAIN LIKE TWAIN

Write a list of clichés. Then create twists that give them new and humorous meanings. Now go and annoy your friends with your new arsenal of witty words.

Mark Twain

"When I was younger I could remember anything, whether it happened or not."

~ Mark Twain

DAY 24
No Pain, No Literary Gain

To make his readers feel sorrow, Twain could open the flood gates of his own personal pain.

When Twain was five, his brother Benjamin died. Years later, before Twain turned twelve, his father also passed away, forcing the family into financial hardship.

After becoming a steamboat pilot on the *Pennsylvania*, Twain secured a job for his younger brother Henry. Three days later, the boat exploded and Twain watched his brother die.

> The brother of Mr. Henry Clemens... hurried to the [Memphis] Exchange to see his brother, and on approaching the bedside of the wounded man, his feelings so much overcame him, at the scalded and emaciated form before him, that he sank to the floor overpowered.
>
> *Memphis Newspaper, 1858*

Later in life, Twain lost a son, two daughters, and his wife, which inspired such tragic work as *The Mysterious Stranger.*

BRAIN LIKE TWAIN

Turn your personal struggles into literary gold. Recall a painful experience and write a page about the ordeal as though it happened to a fictitious character. Make us feel your sorrow through their actions and speech.

Mark Twain

"Nothing helps scenery like ham and eggs."

~ Mark Twain

Twain's Moody Side

Although the nighttime settings in *Huckleberry Finn* were historically accurate, since a boy and fugitive slave would certainly travel under the cover of darkness, this theme also set the mood.

First of all, the night symbolized the dark plague of slavery and the dark conscience of society regarding this matter. As Leslie A. Fiedler observed in an essay, *Tom Sawyer* and *Huckleberry Finn* are "the same dream dreamed twice over, the second time as nightmare."

Secondly, darkness offers an inherent association with the unknown, the forbidden, and the irrational –helping Twain define the "deeper psychology" of evil or simple wrongdoing.

Finally, in contrast with the daylight, Twain jolted his audience when he raised various moral issues.

> Whenever the light of day reveals that evil is the consequence...Huck Finn...comes to make a "judgment of regret."
>
> *Christopher Sten*
> *The Nighttime World of Huck Finn*

BRAIN LIKE TWAIN

Take one of the previous assignments, or a story you've been writing, and do a rewrite, focusing only on the mood. Instead of weather, find other ways to convey your message: maybe the texture of buildings or style of clothing.

Mark Twain

"There are many humorous things in the world; among them the white man's notion that he is less savage than the other savages."

~ *Mark Twain*

DAY 26
Ironing Out Your Irony

Irony was one of Twain's greatest weapons.

In *Huckleberry Finn,* Twain's main character must make a decision "to go to hell" rather than allowing society to force Jim back into slavery. Although society adhered to a strict moral code, they somehow justified their "pro-slavery" sentiment.

In a story about his own military experience, Twain hits on the true irony of war.

> I could not drive it away, the taking of that unoffending life seemed such a wanton thing. And it seemed the epitome of war; that all war must be just that – the killing of strangers against whom you feel no personal animosity; strangers whom, in other circumstances, you would help if you found them in trouble, and who would help you if you needed it. My campaign was spoiled.
>
> *The Private History of a Campaign That Failed*

BRAIN LIKE TWAIN

Have a character make a decision that contradicts their personal sense of morality. *[For example, a politician conceding an election he fraudulently won; or a mugger giving back money to an old lady so she can pay rent.]*

Mark Twain

"Soap and education are not as sudden as a massacre, but they are more deadly in the long run."
~ Mark Twain

Exaggerating to Make a Point

Aside from his *Petrified Man* mentioned earlier, Twain created many far-fetched stories as a news reporter in Nevada.

In *The Empire City Massacre*, which he "swore" was real, a vicious character slaughters his family, and then rides into town with his neck slit open. It kept many people off the street the week it was published.

In *Innocents Abroad,* Twain launched twisted observations at the sacred customs, towns, and art of the Old World:

> [Venice] looked so like an overflowed Arkansas town...I could not get rid of the impressions ...that the river would fall in a few weeks and leave a dirty high-water mark on the houses, and the street full of mud and rubbish."
>
> *Innocents Abroad*

BRAIN LIKE TWAIN

Taking something simple from your daily life, write a few paragraphs and exaggerate the incident to the point of absurdity.

[AUTHOR'S NOTE: If you're doing this at work, we suggest you do not describe your boss as a fire-breathing dragon determined to melt the polar ice cap with his flames and neurotic disposition.]

Mark Twain

"I did not attend his funeral, but I sent a nice letter saying I approved of it."

~ *Mark Twain*

DAY 28

Dialing in Your Dialogue

Dialogue should be as descriptive as prose, painting an accurate portrait of the characters so the reader can visualize the verbal exchange in their mind.

Each voice should be distinct and reveal mood, attitude and education. Their pauses, mannerisms and even choice of words must be well-calculated.

Although Mark Twain was famous for creating realistic dialect, most writers should apply tremendous caution in this area.

> What is known as "dialect" writing looks simple and easy, but is not. It is exceedingly difficult; it has rarely been done well.
>
> *Mark Twain*
> *American Monthly, 1880*

To capture the essence of your characters, observe people with similar backgrounds. Record fragments of dialogue in your mind. Even repeat certain phrases out loud to fully immerse yourself in the lives of these individuals.

This page is too short for sample dialogue, so study Twain's stories such as *How I Edited an Agricultural Paper Once*.

BRAIN LIKE TWAIN

Listen to two people talking. Then try to recreate a portion of their discussion in one page of dialogue.

Mark Twain

"Man is the Reasoning Animal. Such is the claim. I think it is open to dispute."

~ Mark Twain

Find Time to Digest

Twain always kept several books in various stages of completion, and added "a few courses of bricks to two or three" every summer, but never knew which ones.

> As long as a book would write itself, I was a faithful and interested amanuensis and my industry did not flag, but the minute that the book tried to shift to my head the labor of contriving its situations [and] inventing its adventures…I dropped it out of my mind. It was by accident that I found out that a book is pretty sure to get tired along about the middle and refuse to go on with its work until its powers and its interest should have been refreshed by a rest and its depleted stock of raw materials reinforced by lapse of time.
>
> *Unmailed Letter, 1887*

Twain made this discovery writing *Tom Sawyer.* He set the project aside for two years, and then "the book went on and finished itself without any trouble."

Huckleberry Finn took seven years to write. After an early attempt, he told a friend, "I like it only tolerably well…[and may] burn the manuscript when it is done."

BRAIN LIKE TWAIN

Take the day off and let your subconscious do the work.

Mark Twain

"Never put off till tomorrow what may be done day after tomorrow."

~ *Mark Twain*

DAY 30

Blocking Out Writer's Block

Writer's block occurs when fear and laziness collide. It has affected authors since the Egyptians created paper. "The scariest moment," noted Stephen King, the master of suspense, "is just before you start writing."

Maybe you need to do more research to build your confidence in the material (Day 7). Maybe you need to go to the gym or take a walk to refocus your mind (Day 10). But usually you just need to sit down and force yourself to write.

> I wrote the rest of *The Innocents Abroad* in sixty days and I could have added a fortnight's labor with the pen and gotten along without the letters [which the book was based on] altogether…I worked every night from eleven or twelve until broad daylight in the morning… the average was more than 3,000 words a day.
> *Autobiography of Mark Twain*

If you're afraid you will write something horrible, chill out. Your first draft is supposed to be pathetic (Day 11).

"Don't get it right," James Thurber noted. "Just get it written."

BRAIN LIKE TWAIN

Let's end your thirty-day session with your most important assignment – a speed test. Write five pages of garbage. Yes! Don't wait for any inspiration, just write. This task will help you master difficult times in the future.

BONUS TIPS

For Chronic Overachievers

Mark Twain

"Truth is the most valuable thing
we have. Let us economize it."
~ Mark Twain

Honesty is the Best Writing Policy

Twain, like the majority of successful authors, wrote his most enduring work from his heart.

Filled with passion, his words were often so descriptive and powerful they could be offensive at times.

After writing *A True Story,* he made sure to inform the editor that the dialect was not meant as humor, which was a popular comic technique in those days.

The story was a serious account about his sister-in-law's maid, who revealed to him that her slave owner sold her family away from her. Years later, during the Civil War, her son's regiment marched through the plantation where she worked.

Moved by the heart wrenching saga, Twain captured the emotion of their reunion with such vivid detail it became his first contribution to the prestigious *Atlantic Monthly.*

His humor, often laced with brutal honesty, captured the essence of the human spirit. Instead of simply describing locations in his travel books, he exposed the realities of the cultures and characters he encountered.

BRAIN LIKE TWAIN

Write a few paragraphs about an embarrassing moment that happened to you. There's a good chance it happened to someone else, whether or not they admit it.

Mark Twain

"You can't depend on your eyes when your imagination is out of focus."

~ *Mark Twain*

Discovering
Hidden Meanings

The Mississippi River played such an important role in Twain's life that he could draw insightful analogies between our lives and the flowing water that vacillated between tranquility and violent bursts of rage.

> [Twain's] piloting knowledge caused his simplistic assumptions about life…to give way to an awareness of the powerful, often contradictory forces at work beneath the illusory surface of things.
>
> *Todd Warren Howard*
> *Mark Twain: People Who Made History*

The World offers many metaphors for life.

For example, nature mirrors our behavior with her beauty and her contrasting, ever-changing moods and uncertainty.

Motivational speakers use sports to symbolize our need to push ourselves to reach our true potential.

Even the fluctuation of the stock market could illustrate the power of luck in our daily lives.

BRAIN LIKE TWAIN

Think about something you know extremely well, and write a paragraph that uses this knowledge as a metaphor for life.

Mark Twain

"My books are water; those of great geniuses are wine. Everybody drinks water."

~ *Mark Twain*

Rejecting Rejection

Twain's stories were usually well received. However, while working for the *San Francisco Morning Call*, he angered city officials with his politically charged articles and the editors fired him.

Ironically, if Twain didn't lose his job, he might not have had such a great career. He ended up at Angel's Camp, where a miner told him the story that inspired *The Celebrated Jumping Frog of Calaveras County.*

> We should be careful to get out of an experience only the wisdom that is in it – and stop there; lest we be like the cat that sits down on a hot stove-lid. She will never sit on a hot stove-lid again – and that is well; but also she will never sit down on a cold one anymore.
> *Following the Equator*

Writers must have thick skin and short memories. Roughly 27 publishers rejected Dr. Seuss, and an editor even told Rudyard Kipling, "I'm sorry Mr. Kipling, but you just don't know how to use the English language."

BRAIN LIKE TWAIN

Recall a time when you had to deal with rejection. Find the humor in it, and write a few pages.

[AUTHOR'S NOTE: If the pain runs deep enough, you may have a hit like Nora Ephron, who wrote the best-selling novel, Heartburn, *after a painful divorce.]*

Mark Twain

"Habit is habit, and not to be flung out the window by any man, but coaxed downstairs a step at a time."

~ Mark Twain

BONUS TIP
4 Devising Devices

Many critics felt the quotes from *Pudd'nhead Wilson's* calendar were merely an extension of the author's personal philosophy – or possibly even his grandiose ego.

The following analysis, however, asserts Twain cleverly used these quotes as a literary device to enhance the tone (as we attempted in each chapter with our corresponding quotes).

> Although many of the aphorisms [quotes] comment upon specific incidents in the story, they do so in varying degrees of obliqueness, often enlarging upon the book's themes in the process... applicable to more than one chapter or perhaps reflect the whole story tonally. At the same time an aphorism may stand on its own as a comment upon the American character or upon existence.
>
> *James E. Caron*
> *Pudd'nhead Wilson's Calendar:*
> *Tall Tales and a Tragic Figure*

Whew! That was a mouthful, but it shows how Twain layered his story with texture critics didn't even notice.

BRAIN LIKE TWAIN

Create your own literary device that conveys the "tone" and/or "theme" of your story without stalling the narrative. *[Maybe a recurring incident or character's unusual habit.]*

Mark Twain

"Grief can take care of itself, but to get the full value of joy you must have somebody to divide it with."

~ Mark Twain

Finding True Romance

A good love story can often increase your potential market and reveal the softer side of your character.

This, in turn, reveals the theme, because it shows us what your character really wants, and how much he or she is willing to sacrifice to get it.

Although many of Twain's stories lacked this element, he showed an inventive flair in *Tom Sawyer.*

After his "fresh-crowned hero fell without firing a shot," Twain lifted Tom's romance with Becky above puppy love.

> ...relying on the concept of the lover in medieval romance literature...a literary device that spelled out the rules by which the courtly lover paid homage to his noble passion for his lady...the lover's longing for the woman is driven by a desire to be united with her in both body and soul, the goal of which is the achievement of moral perfection.
>
> *Bloom's Major Novelists*

BRAIN LIKE TWAIN

Place your character in King Arthur's court. Either have a knight saving a princess, or to modernize it, make the princess save the knight. Mix romance with adventure, so it appeals to men and women.

Mark Twain

"Civilization is a limitless multiplication of unnecessary necessities."

~ Mark Twain

Your Organized Mess

There are many differences between those who succeed and those who don't, but the ability to keep your work organized improves your odds.

First, you should organize each of your stories before you begin writing (Day 8). Then, as you create more stories, you should maintain a convenient filing system to keep track of your masterpieces.

Twain called this pigeonholing. By keeping his notes and incomplete work in separate compartments, he could find them easily when he wished to return to a specific project.

Computers certainly offer a great system for organizing material. However, until you can transfer your notes to bytes and pieces on your computer, you should keep physical files for your random thoughts (Day 2).

As we learned earlier (Day 28), Twain pigeonholed *Huck Finn* a couple times. Thankfully, he was organized enough to find the manuscript later and transform American literature.

BRAIN LIKE TWAIN

Take thirty minutes to organize your work space.

[AUTHOR'S NOTE: Although the chore may seem overwhelming, dedicate thirty minutes a week to this task, and you may uncover some important documents.]

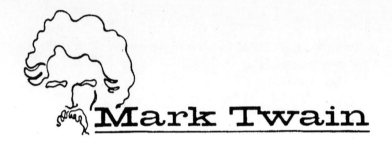

Mark Twain

"Whenever you find yourself on the side of the majority, it is time to pause and reflect."

~ Mark Twain

Know Your Market

Something that entertains one reader may offend another.

While giving a speech at a dinner for the *Atlantic Monthly*, Twain recited a tale about a miner who suspected him of being an imposter posing as a writer.

According to the story, this miner had been deceived by Ralph Waldo Emerson, Henry Longfellow, and Oliver Wendell Holmes, three legendary authors who were sitting in the audience as Twain spoke.

"His satirical subtext was clear to the majority of the audience," noted Todd Warren Howard, "Emerson, Longfellow, and Holmes were literary phonies."

The audience was mortified. Except for one person, who responded with sporadic laughter, the room fell silent.

Hoping to avoid literary persecution, Twain wrote letters to Emerson, Longfellow and Holmes begging forgiveness. In his autobiography, though, Twain admitted he always felt that speech was one of his funniest.

BRAIN LIKE TWAIN

Think of a time when somebody was offended by something you said or wrote or even did. Think about why they might have been upset, and write a paragraph defending *their* point of view.

Mark Twain

"He is now fast rising from affluence to poverty."

~ *Mark Twain*

8

Don't Miss Your Mark Like Mark

After losing his father, Twain grew up in relative poverty and those painful memories haunted him into adulthood. When he became an accomplished author, he resorted to extravagant spending to prove his status, and his monthly expenses were enormous.

Although he was financially secure from the profits generated by his books, some sources suggest he wanted absolute security and no amount of money could satisfy such an insatiable craving. So he indulged in ruinous speculating.

He invested in various businesses, including the creation of a printing press he was certain would make him rich. His publishing company failed, and then the economy collapsed.

To battle bankruptcy (and save his wife from public humiliation), Twain was forced to do a worldwide speaking tour late in life.

BRAIN LIKE TWAIN

Don't wait for your first check as a writer. Open an IRA today and avoid the uncertainty Twain experienced.

*[AUTHOR'S NOTE: Invest $100 a month in a ROTH IRA at a 10% average return each year, and you could have close to a million dollars in roughly 40 years.]**

** DISCLAIMER: Returns will vary, but you should have more money when you retire than you would if you spent it all, right?*

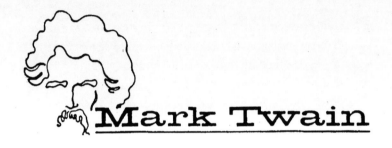

Mark Twain

"Eloquence is the essential thing in a speech, not information."
                            ~ Mark Twain

From Public Nuisance to Public Speaking

Growing up along the Mississippi, Twain was exposed to a variety of talented speakers, including slick-talking salesmen and animated preachers telling tall tales.

> Preparation for Mark Twain's career as a public speaker came...primarily through his exposure to a number of exceptionally able raconteurs and his own gradual absorption of their skills.
>
> *Fred W. Lorch*
> *The Trouble Begins At Eight*

Shortly after moving to Nevada, Twain expanded his knowledge about public performances when his newspaper assigned him to write a report on Artemus Ward, a popular humorist appearing at the local theater.

Observing his dead-pan facial expressions, Twain noticed Ward could get more mileage out of a joke when he pretended he didn't even know he had said anything funny. Twain also learned the power of the pause. "The wait," he wrote in his memoirs, "was more important than the joke."

"Manner is everything," Twain noted after observing a preacher captivate an audience in Brooklyn.

BRAIN LIKE TWAIN

Writers must often promote their own books. So join *Toastmasters* and practice your public speaking.

Mark Twain

"In all matters of opinion, our adversaries are insane."

~ Mark Twain

Criticizing the Critics

When *Huckleberry Finn* was first published, the Concord Library of Massachusetts banned the book because of its corrupting influence over the youth.

> They expelled Huck Finn…as 'trash suitable only for the slums.' That will sell 25,000 copies for us sure.
> *Twain's Letter to His Publisher*

In another part of town, the Concord Free Trade Club took advantage of the publicity to name Twain an honorary member, but the press was not so kind.

The few editors who actually reviewed the book seemed to agree Twain's career as a writer was done. *Life Magazine* stated the book's "blood curdling humor" and "coarse and dreary fun" were unsuitable for children.

> It is the will of God that we must have critics, and missionaries, and Congressmen, and humorists, and we must bear the burden.
> *Autobiography of Mark Twain*

BRAIN LIKE TWAIN

Using Twain's pointed, sardonic and irreverent style, criticize a critic's review. No, not their opinion, but their actual writing style.

[AUTHOR'S NOTE: It's something Twain might have done.]

Your Official
Mark Twain Scorecard

1835   Mark Twain is born in Florida, Missouri. Halley's Comet appears in the sky.

1839   His family moves to Hannibal, Missouri.

1847   His father dies. Twain must get a job as a printer's assistant. He publishes his first story at the age of 12.

1853   He leaves Hannibal and becomes a journeyman printer in St. Louis, New York and Philadelphia.

1857   Twain becomes a steamboat pilot apprentice.

1858   He secures a job for his brother Henry on the steamboat *Pennsylvania*. His brother dies when the ship explodes three days later.

1861   Civil War breaks out. Steamboat traffic stops on the Mississippi, forcing Twain out of a job. His brief stint in the Confederate Army would later inspire his short story, *The Private History of a Campaign That Failed*.

1862   Shortly after moving to Nevada with his brother Orion, he becomes a newspaper reporter for the *Territorial Enterprise* because he fails as a miner.

1864   He moves to San Francisco and begins writing for the *Morning Call*.

1865   The *New York Saturday Press* publishes Twain's *Celebrated Jumping Frog of Calaveras County*.

1866   While visiting Hawaii, Twain writes travel articles for the *Sacramento Union*. When he returns, his humorous lectures become extremely popular.

TWAIN'S BEST-SELLING BOOKS

1869 *Innocents Abroad*, Twain's first travel book, becomes a bestseller.
1872 *Roughing It* offers a humorous account of his days out West.
1873 *The Gilded Age* becomes Twain's first novel, and becomes a successful stage play in New York.
1876 *The Adventures of Tom Sawyer*
1880 *A Tramp Abroad*
1882 *The Prince and the Pauper*
1883 *Life on the Mississippi*
1885 *Adventures of Huckleberry Finn*
1889 *A Connecticut Yankee in King Arthur's Court*
1894 *Pudd'nhead Wilson*

TRAGEDY STRIKES TWAIN & HIS FAMILY

1895 Mark Twain begins his round-the-world lecture tour to pay off his debts.
1896 His daughter Susy dies of meningitis while Twain is in Europe. Twain is devastated.
1898 He finishes paying off his creditors.
1904 His wife Livy dies.
1909 His youngest daughter Jean dies, suffering from an epileptic seizure on Christmas Eve.
1910 Mark Twain dies as Halley's Comet appears: "I came in with Halley's Comet…and I expect to go out with it… The Almighty has said, no doubt: Now here are these two unaccountable freaks; they came in together, they must go out together."

Your Author
&
Mark Twain Tour Guide

David Andrew Lloyd writes comedy – because that's all he can take seriously.

While studying Mark Twain at Purdue University, Lloyd learned to appreciate the true power of satire. His humorous stories, essays and letters have appeared in *National Lampoon, American Legion, Poker Digest, USA Today,* and *Advertising Age* to name a few.

As an award-winning screenwriter, he has sold and optioned scripts to *Fox/Searchlight, Franchise Pictures* and several other production entities.

In a crusade against the senseless abuse of the adverb, Lloyd wrote *Brain Like Twain* to help other writers reach their full potential by using the secrets of one of America's greatest literary minds.

Printed in Great Britain
by Amazon.co.uk, Ltd.,
Marston Gate.